Mark

The Realist Years : Selected Works

Rothko

Essay by: Klaus Kertess

October 31, 2001 – January 05, 2002

32 East 57th Street, New York City

PaceWildenstein

City Light

By Klaus Kertess

The work Mark Rothko created in the 1930s literally and figuratively precedes the name he claimed for himself. Hindsight often makes an artist's development too orderly and urges formative work into a seamless narrative culminating in a signature style. Rothko's early paintings no more forecast the radiant rectangular nimbuses inhabiting his painted planes from 1949 until his death in 1970 than do Pablo Picasso's so-called Blue Period paintings forecast the planar atomizations of Cubism undertaken a decade later in 1910. Like such peers as Jackson Pollock and Clyfford Still, Rothko moved through the gummy straits of American Regionalism and Social Realism toward a goal he could hardly have perceived in 1930. His mentor Milton Avery and his friend Adolph Gottlieb, as well as Giorgio de Chirico, Edvard Munch, fifteenth-century Italian Renaissance portraiture, John Marin, and Max Ernst contributed to the countercurrents of Rothko's development. And, yes, clues and evidence exist that point to the ultimate acts: inward stillness, dislocation, preoccupation with planar architecture; suffused, occasionally smoldering light.

Estrangement and anxiety colored Rothko's life and early art. Speaking no English, the Russian-born, ten-year-old Marcus Rothkowitz arrived in Portland, Oregon, with his mother and sister in 1913 to join his father, who had emigrated three years earlier. English was not taught in the first grade of the school he attended. His father died in 1914. Happiness didn't figure in his youth, nor did art. Rothkowitz attended Yale University for two years (1922-23) without enrolling in any art classes. Briefly, he took a drawing class at the Art Students League in 1924 before returning to Portland to study acting. After coming back to New York a year later and being refused a scholarship to learn acting, he enrolled again at the Art Students League and studied with Max Weber (1925-26). Weber had been one of the earliest American converts to Cubism and a major messenger of modernism in New York, although he had now turned to more expressionistic figuration. Via Weber, Rothkowitz learned the lessons of Cézanne. However, his friendship with the older Milton Avery proved to be the more catalytic event of his early development.

Avery had arrived in New York from Connecticut in 1925 and quickly shed his American Impressionist beginnings and enthusiastically embraced the flatness and saturated colors of Matisse and the Fauves, merging them with the ebullient plainness of much American folk art. Rothkowitz met Avery and his wife, Sally, through an old friend from Portland in 1928, and they began to see each other regularly. The almost perennially happy Connecticut Yankee and the almost perennially alienated Russian immigrant formed a critical nexus in the development of American modernism of the second quarter of the twentieth century. In 1929, Rothkowitz introduced Avery to his new friend, Adolph Gottlieb, and they were occasionally joined by Barnett Newman and John Graham.

The acutely calibrated, flat planar organics of Avery's compositions, as well as his increasingly thinned-down layers of paint, which simulated the transparency of watercolor and drew an overall suffused light up to the surface from layers below, encouraged a newly assured compositional simplicity and layered painterly variegation in Rothkowitz's paintings. However, Avery's lyric refinement, wit, and deep commitment to landscape couldn't be further removed from the dark vapors of urban estrangement that envelop Rothkowitz's paintings of the 1930s. Claustrophobic enigmas such as *Lesson* (1932-33) look more to Édouard Vuillard's compressed domestic interiors and to Rembrandt's simmering butterscotch surfaces than to Avery's breezy openness.

In 1932, Rothkowitz, his new wife, Edith, and the Gottliebs spent their summer vacation together in Cape Ann, Massachusetts, near the Averys, whom they often visited in Gloucester. The rare, for Rothkowitz, subject of bathers seen in *Untitled (Two Nudes)* (1933-34) shows us that none of Rothkowitz's anxiety evaporated by the sea. The painting's very high horizon, lack of local detail, and monumental, pared down central nude call to Avery; but even Avery's darker, more mysterious paintings such as *Card Players* (1934) still endow his bathers with a pneumatic grace and repose unknown to the crunched bundle of nerves trapped in the center of Rothkowitz's beach. And the nude's discomfort is bared not by moonlight but by some urban subterranean glare. Edvard Munch's traumatized muteness might have played some role here.

Throughout the 1930s, Rothkowitz continued to paint dark interior-exterior architectural spaces confined in shallow rectangularity and inhabited by one to three figures immobilized in traumatized stillness. Some of these dark toned urban trances, such as *Untitled (Two Seated Women)* (1933-34; plate 1) call to the grittier and more outwardly socially conscious works of the Ashcan School; others, such as *Untitled (Three Women)* (c. 1935), burden the carefree amplitude of Avery's color and figures with dour angst. The more surreal fragmentations and mutations Picasso began inflicting upon his figures after 1925, including the cannibalistic ferocity of the two heads in *The Kiss* (1931), seep through the melancholy embrace of Rothkowitz's *Untitled (Couple Kissing)* (1934-35; plate 5).

None of these paintings is a mere pastiche. Avery's figures are posed and poised in curvilinearity. Rothkowitz's figures hover in an awkward blockiness, at once alien to and trying to assimilate the rectangularity of their support. The canvas plane emits a subdued flicker of electric light rising through the visibly brushstroked layers of thin paint that simultaneously blurs and defines the shadowy figures. Rothkowitz achieved a kind of veiled expressionism that roiled the surface with slow motion displacement both physical and psychological. The light radiating from below and the shifting compositional play with the canvas plane's rectangularity coalesce into an eerie poetics of placelessness. At the same time Rothkowitz was assimilating Avery, along with Rembrandt and post-Cubist Picasso, Pollock was assimilating the lessons of his teacher, Thomas Hart Benton, and of Albert Pynkham Ryder and El Greco, into paintings more viscerally agitated than those of Rothkowitz. More than a decade would still separate each from his stunning breakthrough.

Rothkowitz's paintings could hardly have been executed during a time other than the Depression; however, the year of the Depression's onset, 1929, also marks the opening of The Museum of Modern Art and the marked increase of New York's role as an art center. While the Modern's agenda was dominated by European modernism and, two years later, the new Whitney Museum of American Art focused on American Regionalist and Social Realist painters largely untainted by European modernism, little attention was spent on local artists struggling to move beyond Social Realism toward modernism. In 1935, Rothkowitz, his friend Gottlieb, Ilya Bolotowsky, and six other artists formed The Ten (although they were only nine) to further their quest for new painting solutions that began to place more emphasis on the metaphysical than the social.

The year 1936 marks the beginning of a greater expansiveness in Rothkowitz's painting—in his handling of paint, color, and composition. Rothkowitz had already been grinding many of his own pigments and now began mixing more white into his thinned layers of paint; variations in transparency and opacity, in visibly brushed and shiny-smooth over texture, in tonal depths, as well as in hues, all merge in glowing penumbral oscillations. Not a natural light, but an interior light, from within the paint, within the mind, within man-made space, hovers in a shimmering blur on the edge of the viewer's focus. In *Self-Portrait* (1936; plate 4), we see the artist's contour emerging from and being eroded by an acidic orange into yellow into ocher into red light. Not the slightest of detail describes his space; only light defines the artist's place. Legs cut off by the bottom of the canvas, one hand folded over the other, he hovers, as stunned into silence as his other subjects. The circles of dark haze serving as Rothkowitz's glasses mediate between our eyes and his. Rothkowitz was afflicted with acute myopia that, without glasses, would cause distant objects to blur because they would focus in front of the retina rather than on it (Pierre Bonnard was similarly afflicted). One can only speculate upon the possible effect of his sight (when uncorrected by glasses) on the embodiment of his vision, but the evading of focus would, of course, help urge the later paintings toward mystery and intangibility.

The bold simplifications and massing of the artist's figure, combined with the large amount of space consumed by the contour, imbue *Self-Portrait* with a new confidence and monumentality—a confidence also visible in the more complex rectangular harmonics with which Rothkowitz scored canvases such as *Untitled (Cityscape)* (c. 1936). This painting and several other contemporaneous ones that conflate interior and exterior city views look to the liquification of Cubism initiated more than twenty years earlier by John Marin. Marin's fame rested on his watercolors, which had been critical to Avery's development and certainly encouraged Rothko's thinning of oil paint and quest for transparency. Marin was perhaps the most ubiquitous and influential of the earlier wave of American modernists. One of the few Americans to be recognized by The Museum of Modern Art, he was given a retrospective there in 1936.

The increasing attention Rothkowitz paid to rectangular measure and the painted interior allusions to and illusions of the physical plane of the canvas is also indebted to the Italian Renaissance—to the architectural framing devices congruent with the support plane employed in so many Italian Renaissance portraits and depictions of the Madonna and Child, from Filippino Lippi in Florence to Titian in Venice. Even the medley of dryly brushed beiges configuring the window frame within the plane of *Untitled (Two Women at a Window)* (c. 1937; plate 6) recalls Florentine masonry. And in his 1936 *Interior*, Rothkowitz riffed on Michelangelo's Laurentian Library, subtracting the curvilinear staircase in order to fuse the architectural articulation with the flat plane of the canvas. The resulting rectangular division does not prefigure the mature work but gives clear evidence of the crucial importance of measure to Rothkowitz and forms another bridge to his subsequent identity as Rothko.

A still living Italian master, Giorgio de Chirico, further altered Rothkowitz's urban perspective. De Chirico arrived for a two-year stay in New York in 1936, the year he was so prominently featured in an exhibition critical to the development of the Abstract Expressionist generation: "Fantastic Art, Dada, and Surrealism" at The Museum of Modern Art. The disjunctive plazas combining radically tilted ramps and mute mannequins as well as nostalgic allusions to Classical myth and culture that filled de Chirico's paintings from 1910 to 1918 had already inspired many of the Surrealists (he was not known in New York until his work started to be exhibited there in 1928). New York City, with its skyscraper Babel of historical styles laid out on a grid, had fueled de Chirico's fantasies long before his arrival; and, now, de Chirico's imaginary vistas began to encourage Rothkowitz to more emphatically distort his observation-dependent vision.

In the sketches Rothkowitz drew in subway stations, he retained the shallow frontal space so prevalent in his work in oil; but, in the paintings of underground subway stations he created between 1937 and 1939, the platform was tilted into more vertiginous perspectival distortion until, in 1939, it became almost vertical. And the figures frozen in anticipation became more generalized, almost wooden in their ashen whiteness. While not nearly so disjunctive and assertively, ambiguously symbolic as a painting like de Chirico's *The Duo* or *The Mannequins of the Rose Tower* (1915; seen in his 1935 Pierre Matisse Gallery exhibition), the haunted nowhereness and vacuous silence of Rothkowitz's subterranean platforms become metaphors for a kind of mental limbo where loss and anticipation are locked in stale- mate. The more willful abstractness and geometric rigor further removes Rothkowitz's work from the more purely Social Realist treatment common to this subject. Walker Evans, like John Sloan and others before him, also turned to the subway; but the remarkable photographs he created between 1938 and 1941 were made not on the platform but inside subway cars with a hidden camera and reflect more readily identifiable urban apprehensions.

Rothkowitz enveloped his above-ground domestic interiors in vapors often as enigmatic as those enfolding his subway underworld. The volumes of the ordinarily dressed couple seen in *Untitled (Standing Man and Woman)* (1938) seem to have been compressed between the foreground of the painting and the rectangular architectural details of the background—looking as if they have been ironed into the architec- ture of the plane to become denizens of rectangularity. Occasionally the figures exceed by far in size and in scale the interiors meant to house them, as does the nude in *Seated Figure* (1939; plate 21). This female fig- ure calls to the often radically overscaled figures in de Chirico's late, fluffy paintings such as *Antique Nudes* (1927; seen in his second New York exhibition at the end of 1928).

And Rothkowitz's subdued color took on more radiance, lightened with white and activated into a glimmering veil by increasingly varied layers of thinly brushed paint, as we can see in the 1938 *Untitled (Seated Woman)* (plate 18). Everything becomes subservient to the creation of light. The brushstroking- drawing maintains a discreet visibility and works primarily to encourage short, irregular, multidirectional strokes to layer into a viscous screen perforated by light. The figure seems to exist primarily as a carrier of light and mediator between mottled red and white. In that half of her on the white side, her dark coat is shot through with a haphazard damask of reddish light; and, on the red side, her coat sparkles with a dew of off-white. Only the foreshortening of the chair legs hints at mimetic space in this flutter of irregular rectangularity.

In January 1940, Marcus Rothkowitz changed his name to Mark Rothko. He had not been able to grow into the three syllables of his birth name, already once transcribed from one alphabet to another. Very early in his life, two uncles had changed their name to Roth and one to Weinstein; and his mother changed her first name from Anna to Kate. Rothko, less ordinary than Roth and unburdened of its ending, which means joke in German, retained some of its immigrant origins while achieving an iconic simplicity, visual and oral. Like his name, the art Rothko began in 1940 marked a new beginning without denying its past.

In 1940, Rothko and Gottlieb saw each other daily and entered into a more urgent dialogue about the direction of their art. As war engulfed Europe, more and more artists rejected political ideals, seeking instead a primal universality—a reaction not uncommon in times of cataclysm. In New York, this turn from world politics to the collective unconscious had already begun in 1939, when the Hitler-Stalin pact made it difficult for Communist sympathizers, including members of The Ten, to maintain political allegiance to the Soviet Union. The left's disillusionment with Communism was then exacerbated by Hitler's maniacal destruction. With the realization that one political system was no different from another, Rothko and Gottlieb, like many of their peers, abandoned the warring world for internal truths, embracing Surrealism's advocacy of the unconscious as the legitimate source of art. They too embarked on a path of destruction—metaphorical destruction and reclamation. Physical observation would be displaced by metaphysical imagining. Both Gottlieb and Rothko sought to retrieve the mythic. Not necessarily specific myths, although each occasionally turned to one, but a retrieval of the embodiment of a mythic consciousness.

Their first forays toward the metaphysical engaged more imagined subjects and imposed more radical distortions on the congruent, stagelike space each had previously employed. Rothko's *Oedipus* (1940) has sprouted multiple profiles and limbs (one arm about to poke an eye out) and looks like a carnivalesque mutant of de Chirico's late classicizing figures. The interior space dissolves in a panoply of rectangularity in harmony with the shape of the painting but mimetically undecipherable. Rothko continued to retain a highly schematized stagelike space, whereas Gottlieb, in 1941, began turning his canvases into irregular grids, each section of which contained a stick figure head or arm or a fish or an eye or a spiral, etc. His Pictographs looked to Paul Klee's childlike simplicities, as well as to the tribal art and cave painting previously so admired by Picasso and the Surrealists and featured in exhibitions at The Museum of Modern Art in 1935 and 1937. Rothko sometimes preferred more classicized distortions, partially in response to his dialogue with Gottlieb, compartmentalizing sections of figures in coffinlike rectangles, as in *Crucifix* (1941-42). The squared-off, morphed together faces seen in *Heads* (1941-42) look as if they grew out of and into the rectangle of the canvas—the subject becomes a culture of the rectangular.

In 1942, bird and vegetal phantasms began to populate Rothko's planes. The two beaked creatures on the right in *Untitled* (1942) look like relatives of Max Ernst's avian monster Loplop; and the figure of Iphigenia in *Sacrifice of Iphigenia* (1942) looks more like a griffin than a human. Clearly Rothko was absorbing more Surrealist fabulism. At the same time, his variegated strokes of paint became lighter in both hue and touch, making his work more translucent and more and more like watercolor. And, indeed, beginning in 1944, watercolor and arabesquing wisps of water creatures would largely fill Rothko's painting and subject it to the sea change that, by the end of the decade, transformed his rectangles into figures of spirit.

Rothko arrived late to painting and to his name. The work he created in the 1930s is filled with an intensity, pathos, and brooding light that embody not only his personal sense of dislocation, but that of much of the population at large during the decade of the Depression. This work also reveals the critical importance of measure, which would continue to figure in Rothko's art throughout his career. It was the city and its kaleidoscopic rectangularity—not landscape—that fueled Rothko's work from the beginning (the tripartite rectangular division so prevalent in Rothko's painting in almost every phase of his work undermines the reading of a landscape horizon). In the 1930s, the rectangle staged the vulnerably mortal figure; in the 1950s, the rectangle became the metaphysically vulnerable figure.

Klaus Kertess is an art critic, fiction writer, and independent curator.

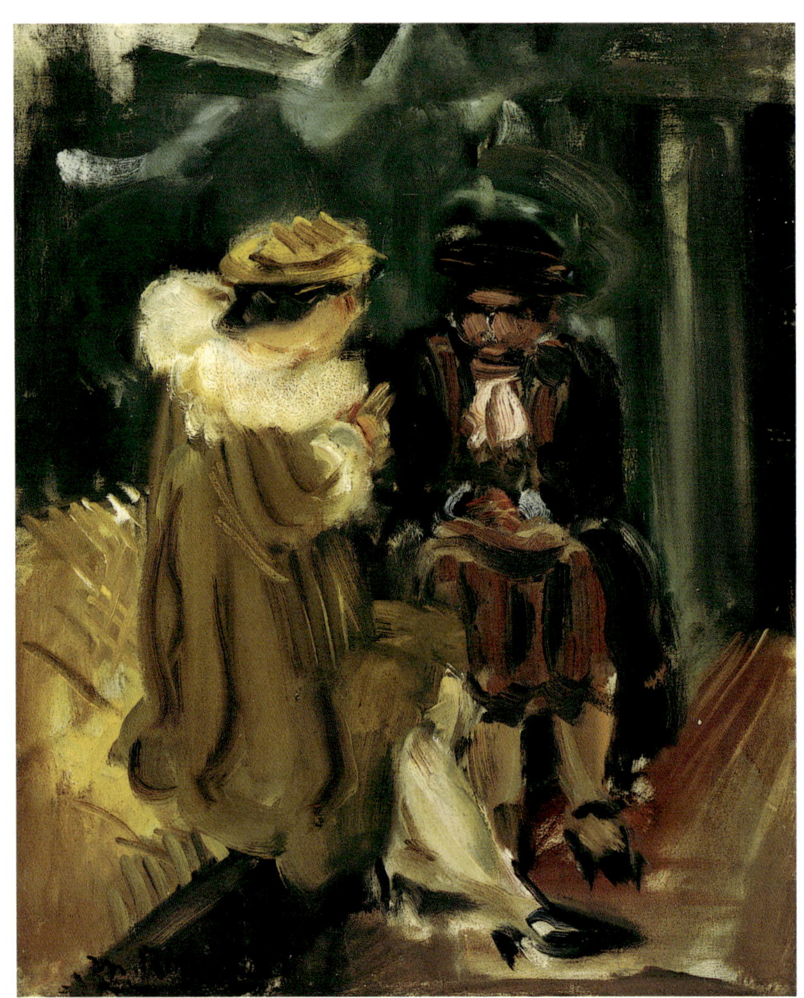

1. Untitled (Two Seated Women), 1933-34
oil on black linen
18 ⅝ x 15 ½"
Lent by the Brooklyn Museum of Art
Gift of The Mark Rothko Foundation, Inc.

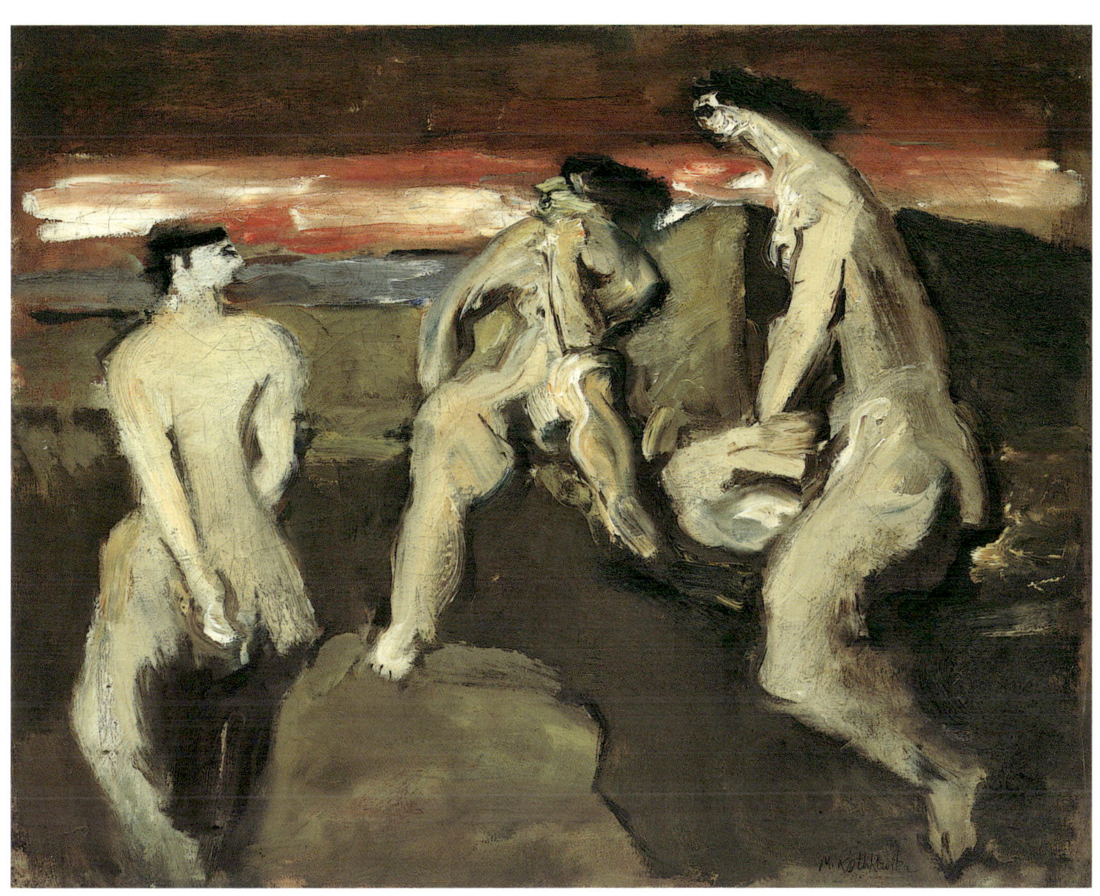

2. Bathers, 1933-34
oil on canvas
21 x 27"

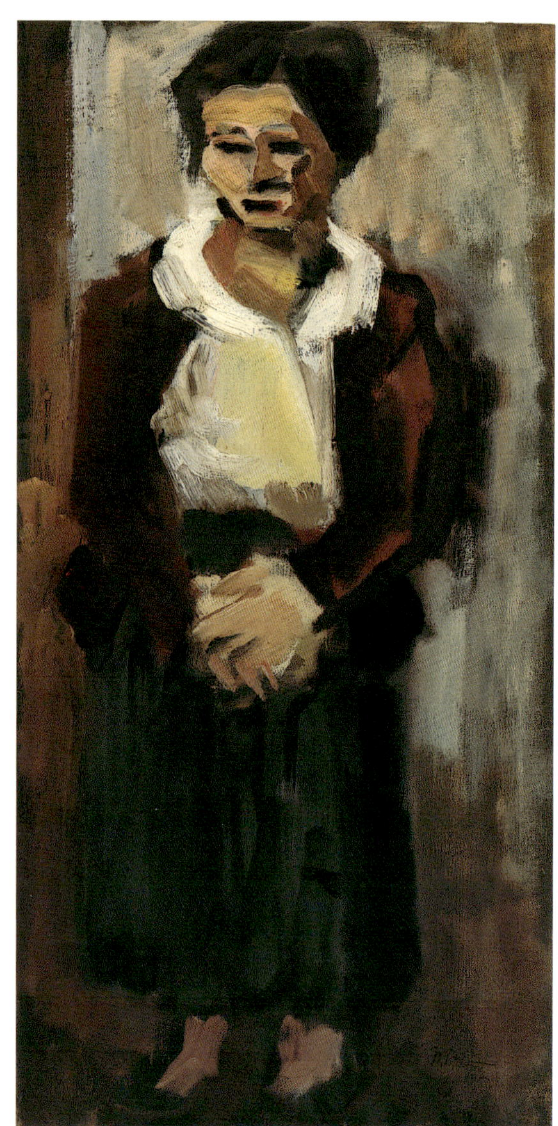

3. The Red Blouse, 1933-34
oil on canvas
31 ½ x 16"

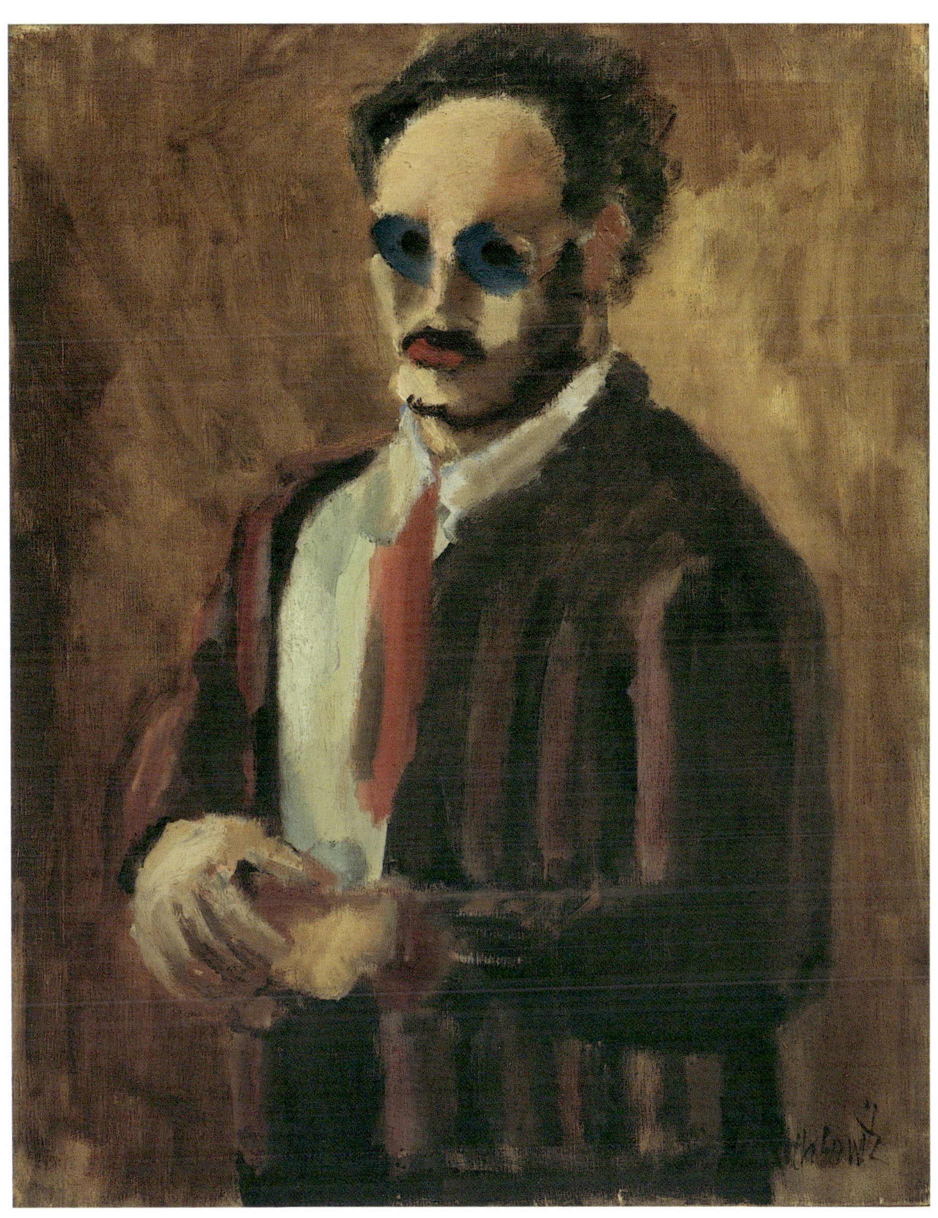

13

4. Self-Portrait, 1936
oil on canvas
32 ¼ x 25 ¾"

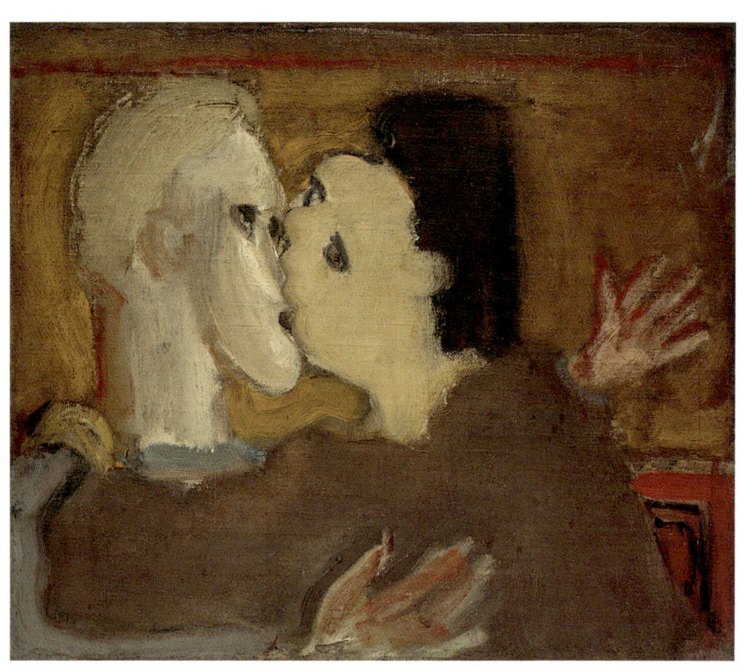

5. Untitled (Couple Kissing), 1934-35
oil on canvas
12 $\frac{1}{8}$ x 14"

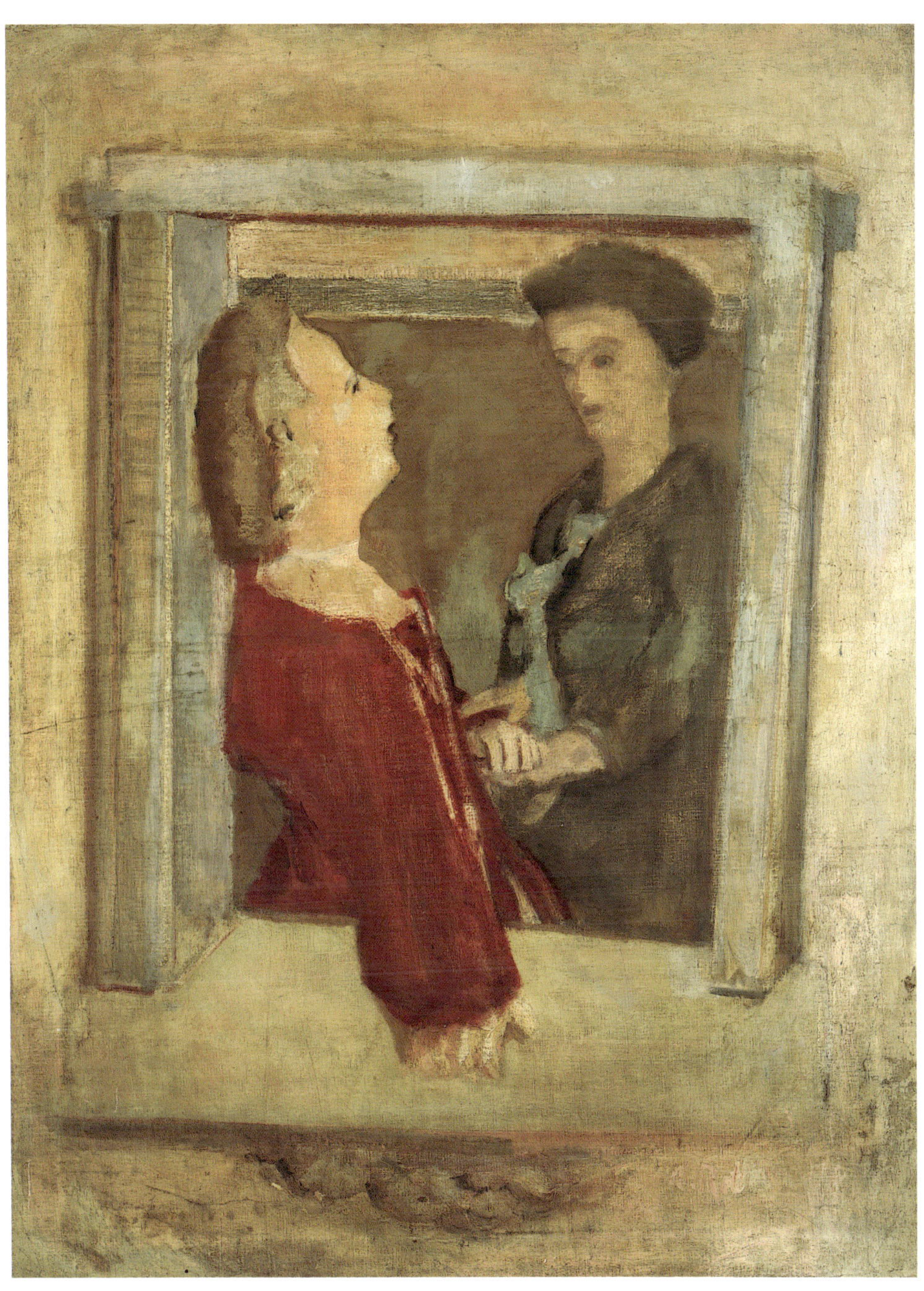

6. Untitled (Two Women at a Window), c.1937
oil on canvas
40 x 30"
Collection of Ira Smolin and Linda Washburn

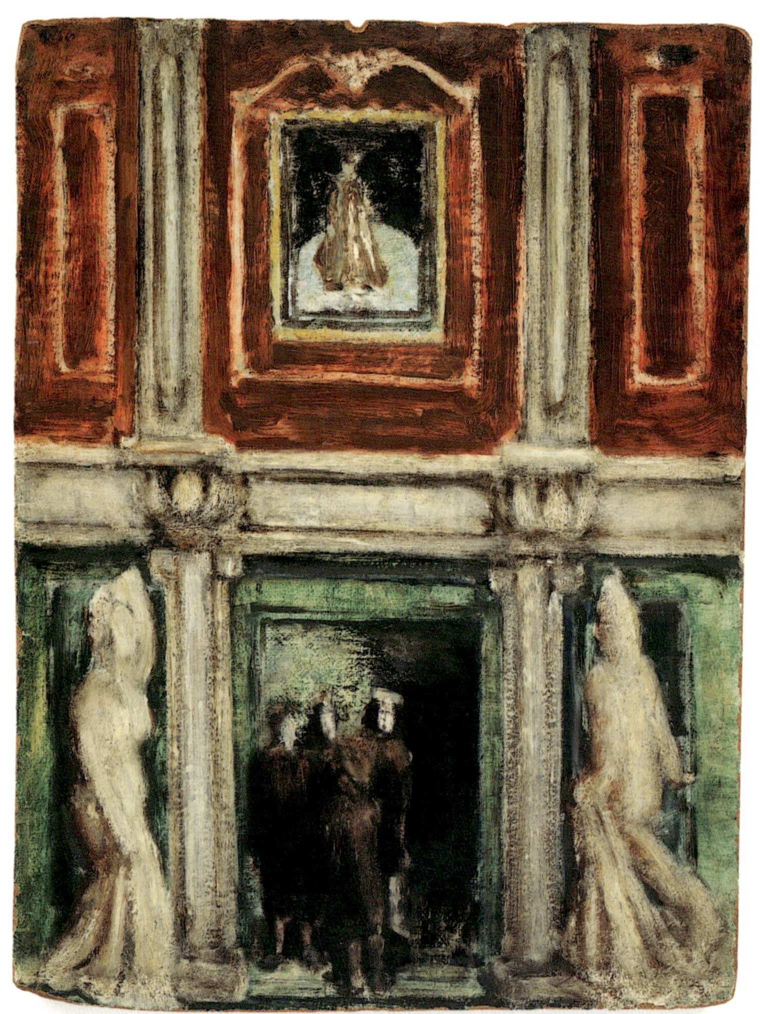

16

7. Interior, 1936
oil on hardboard
23 7/8 x 18 1/4"
National Gallery of Art, Washington
Gift of The Mark Rothko Foundation, Inc.

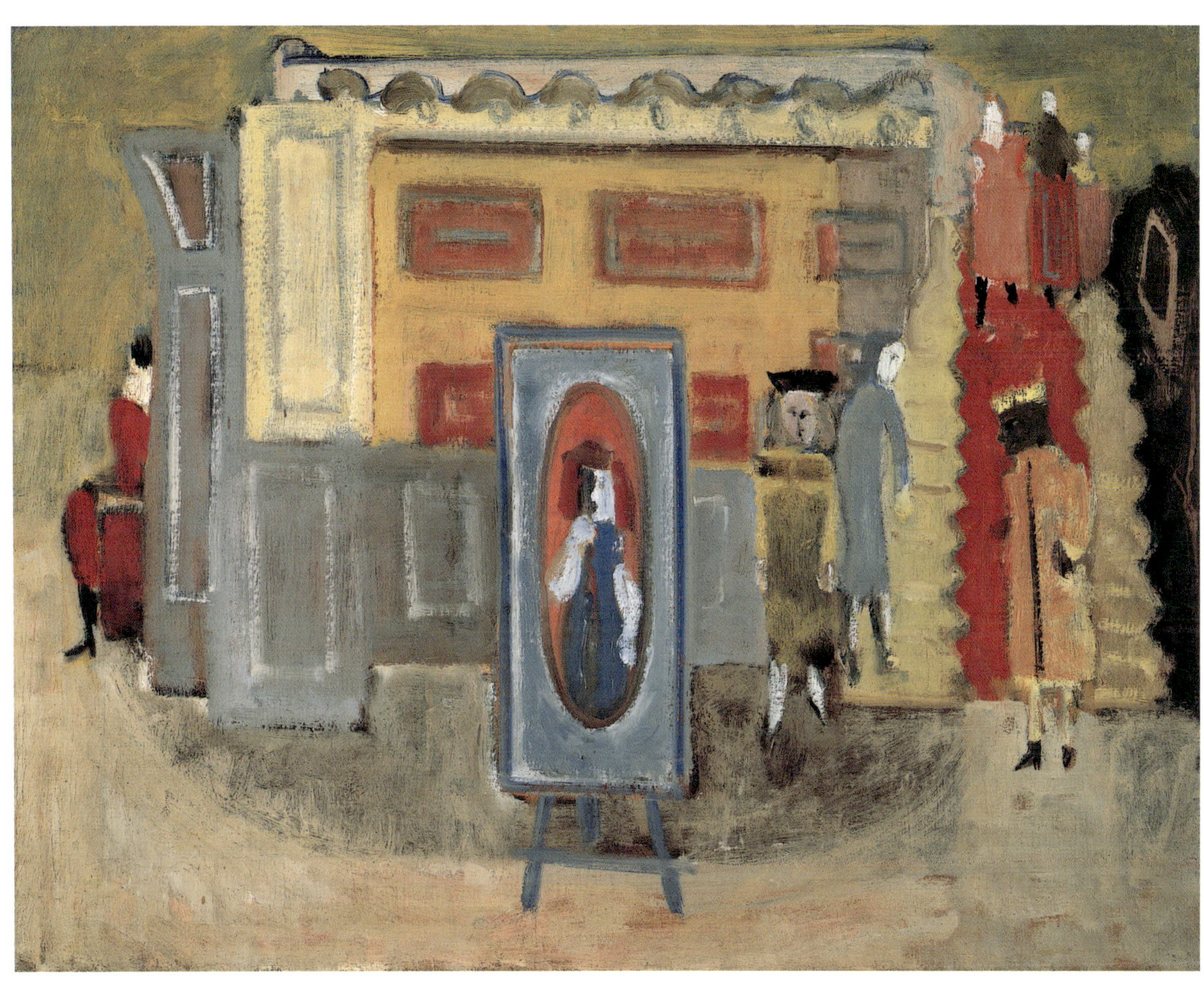

8. Untitled (Lobby/Restaurant), 1936-37
oil on canvas
28 x 36"

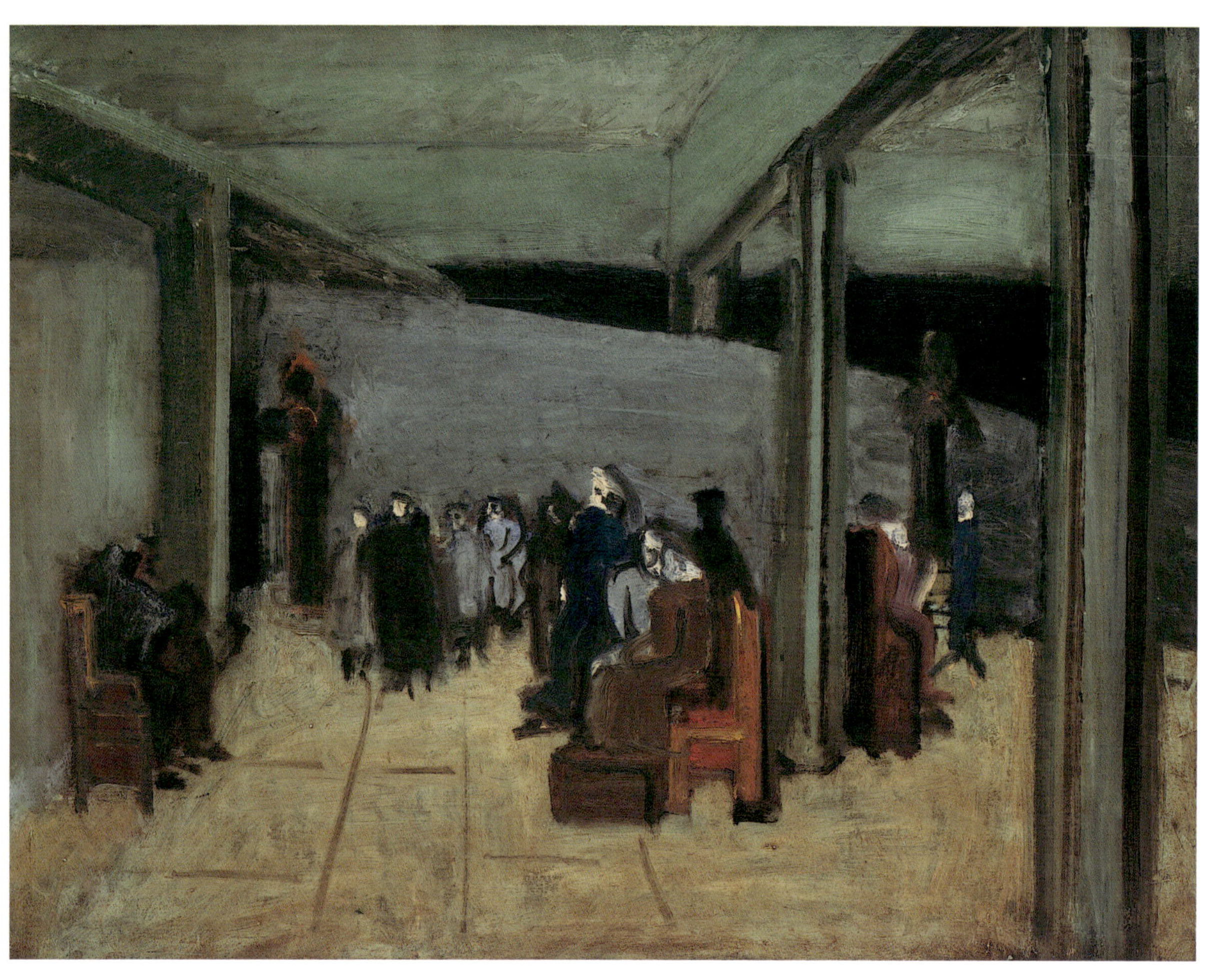

18

9. Untitled (Waiting Room), 1935
oil on canvas
32 ³/₈ x 42"

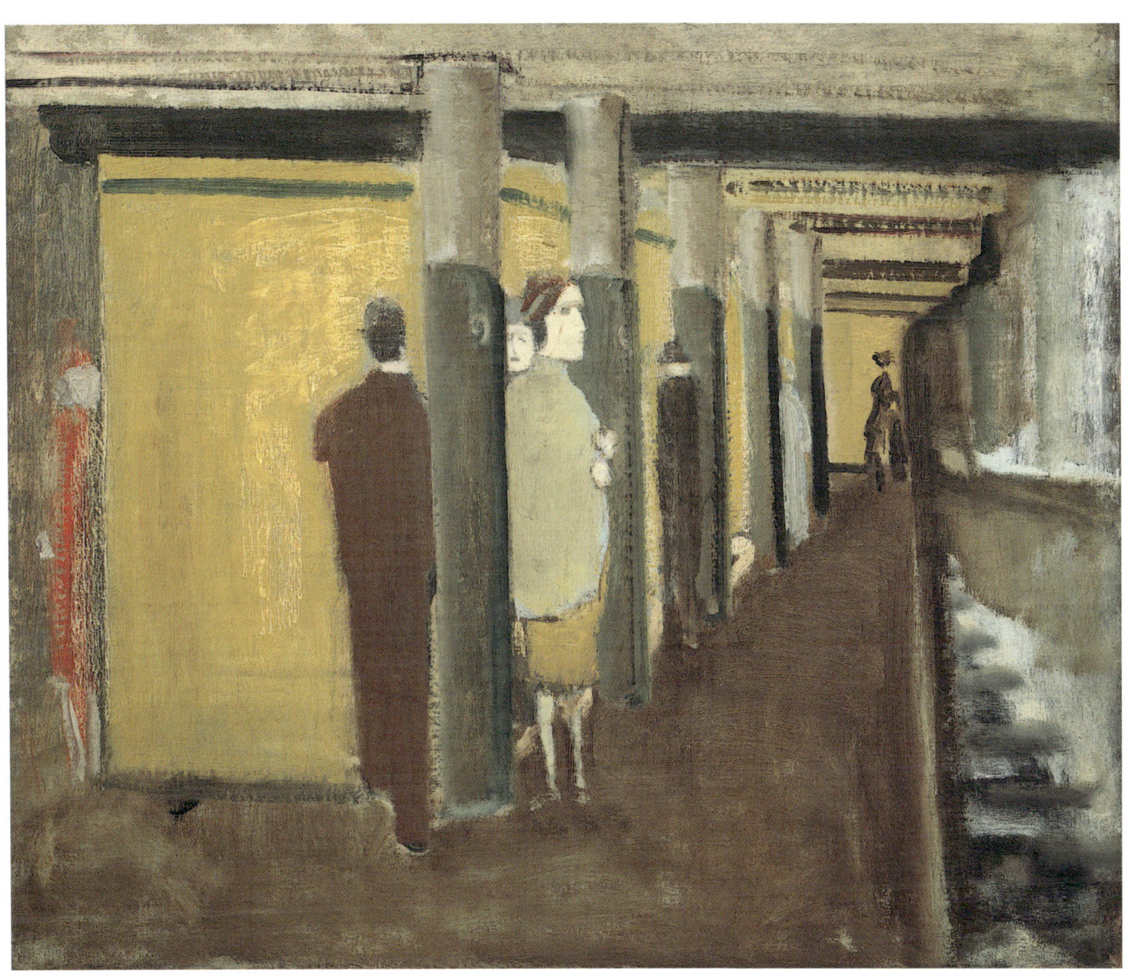

10. Subway, c. 1937
oil on canvas
29 ⁷⁄₈ x 35 ⁷⁄₈"

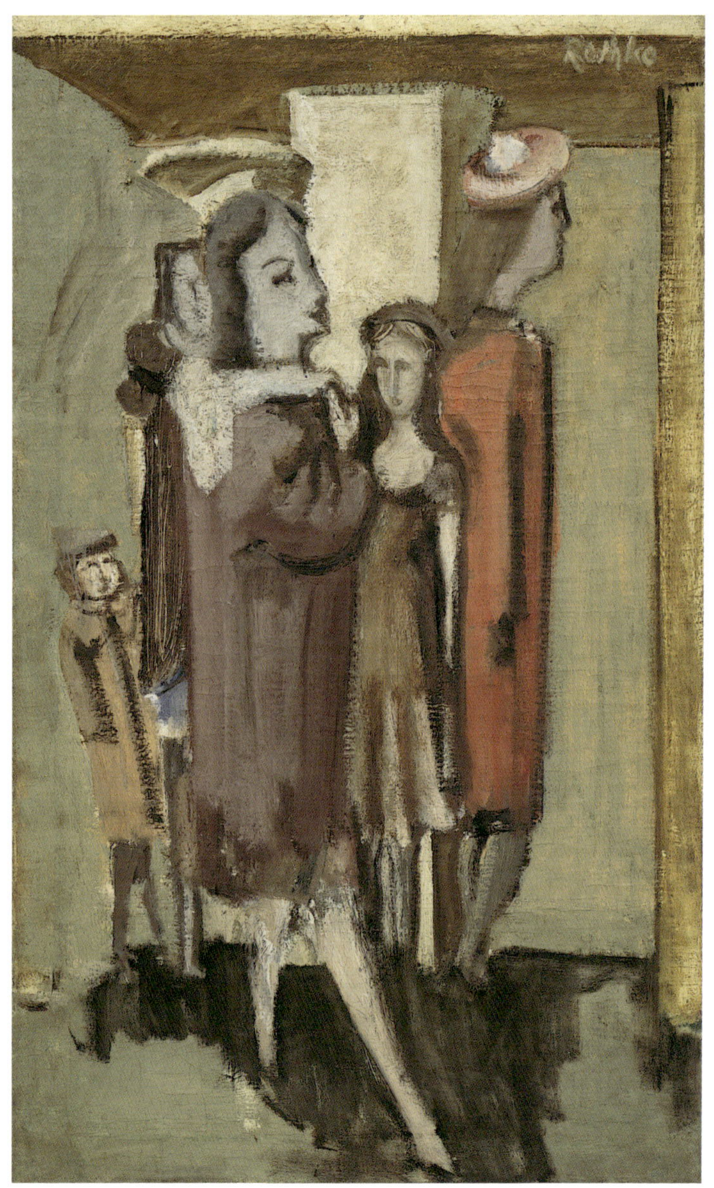

11. Metropolitan Scene, 1934-36
oil on canvas
36 x 22"

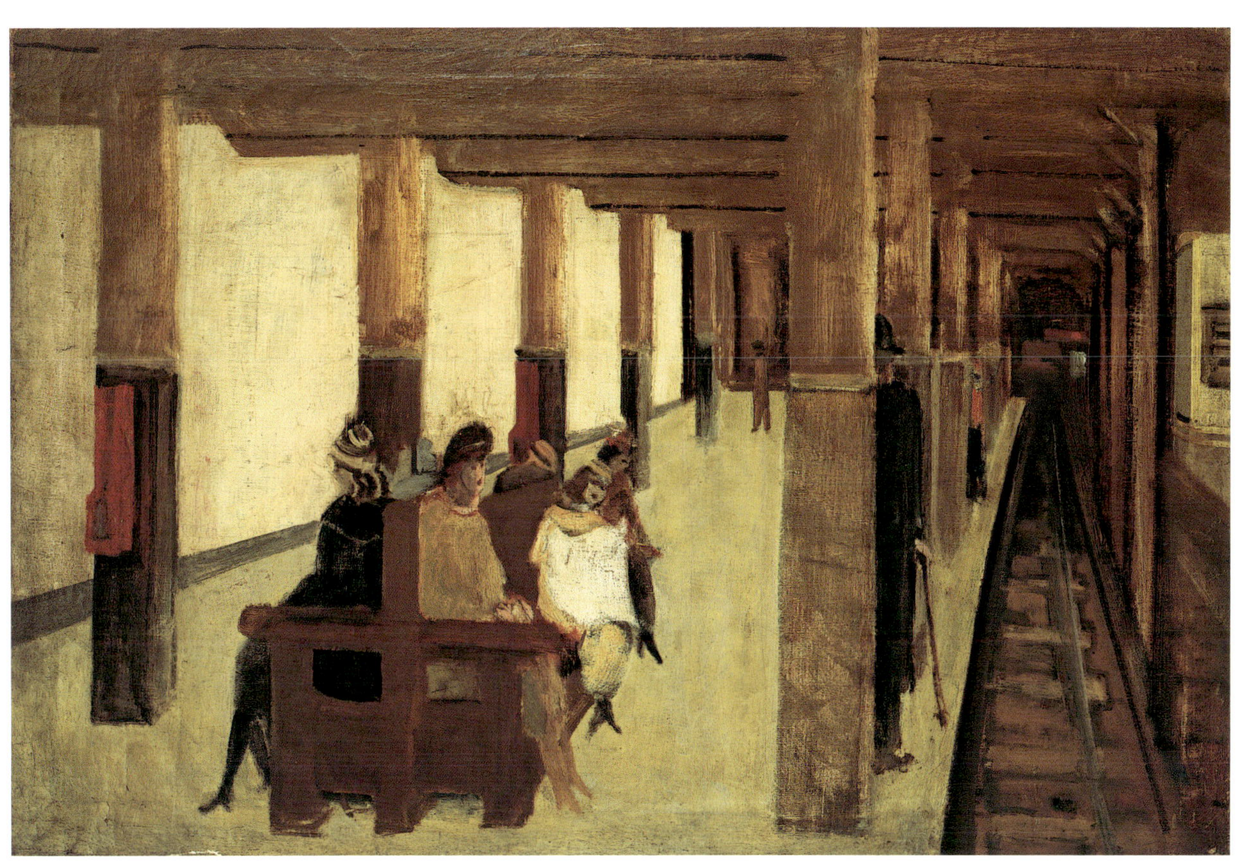

12. Untitled (Subway), 1937
oil on canvas
24 x 36"
Collection of Ira Smolin and Linda Washburn

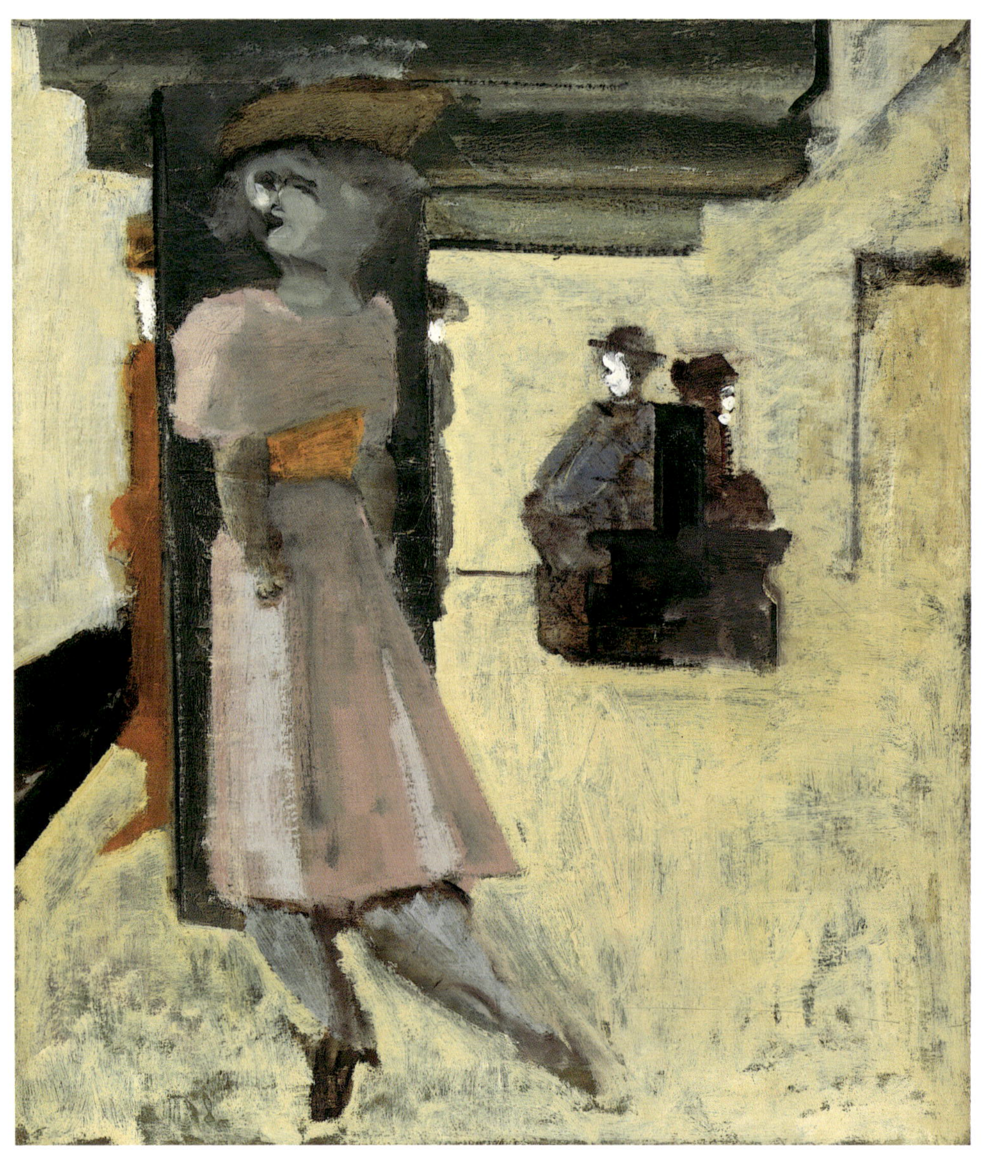

22

13. Subway, 1938-39
oil on canvas
34 ¼ x 29 ⅞"

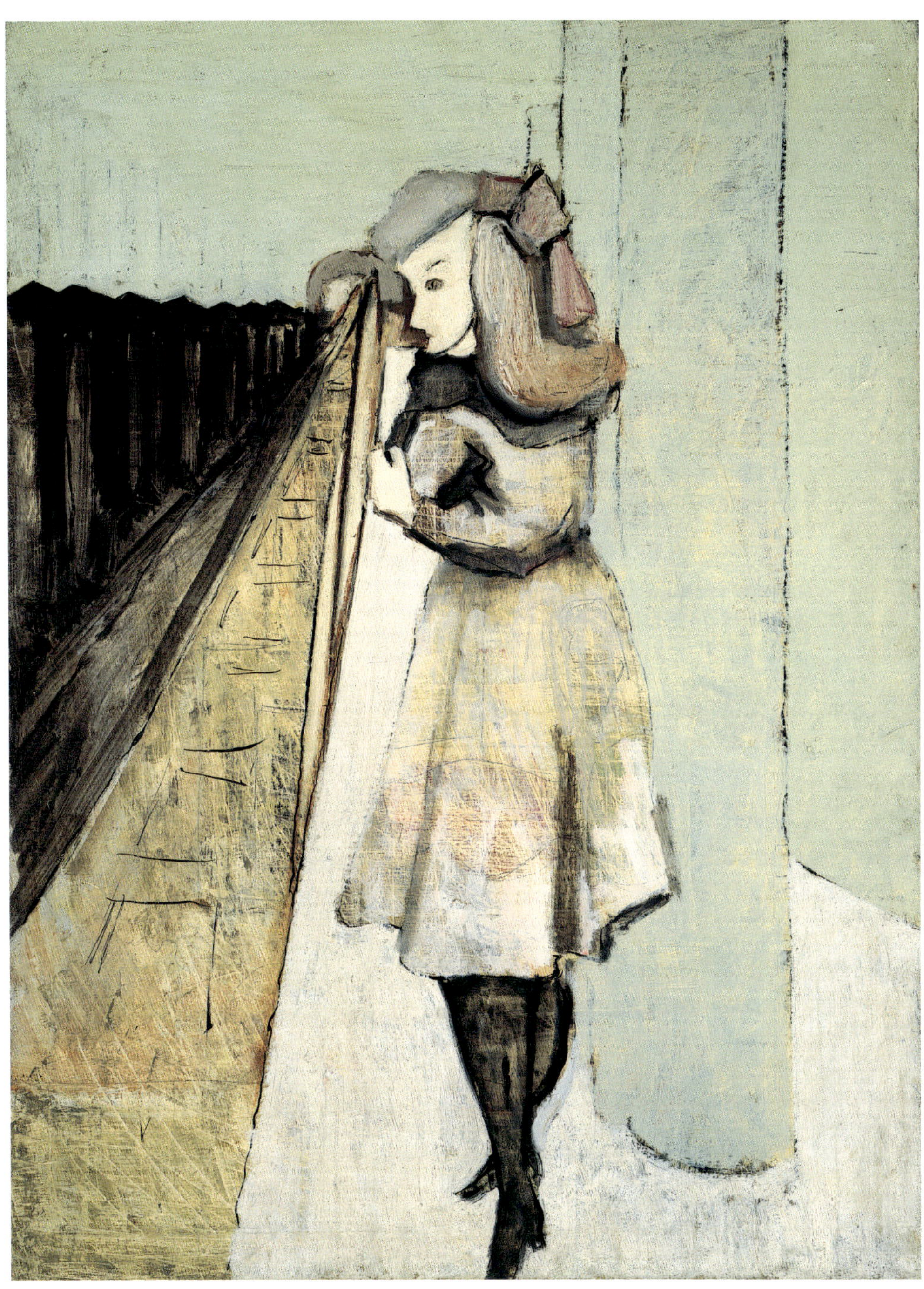

14. Untitled (Woman in Subway), c. 1938
oil on canvas
40 x 30"

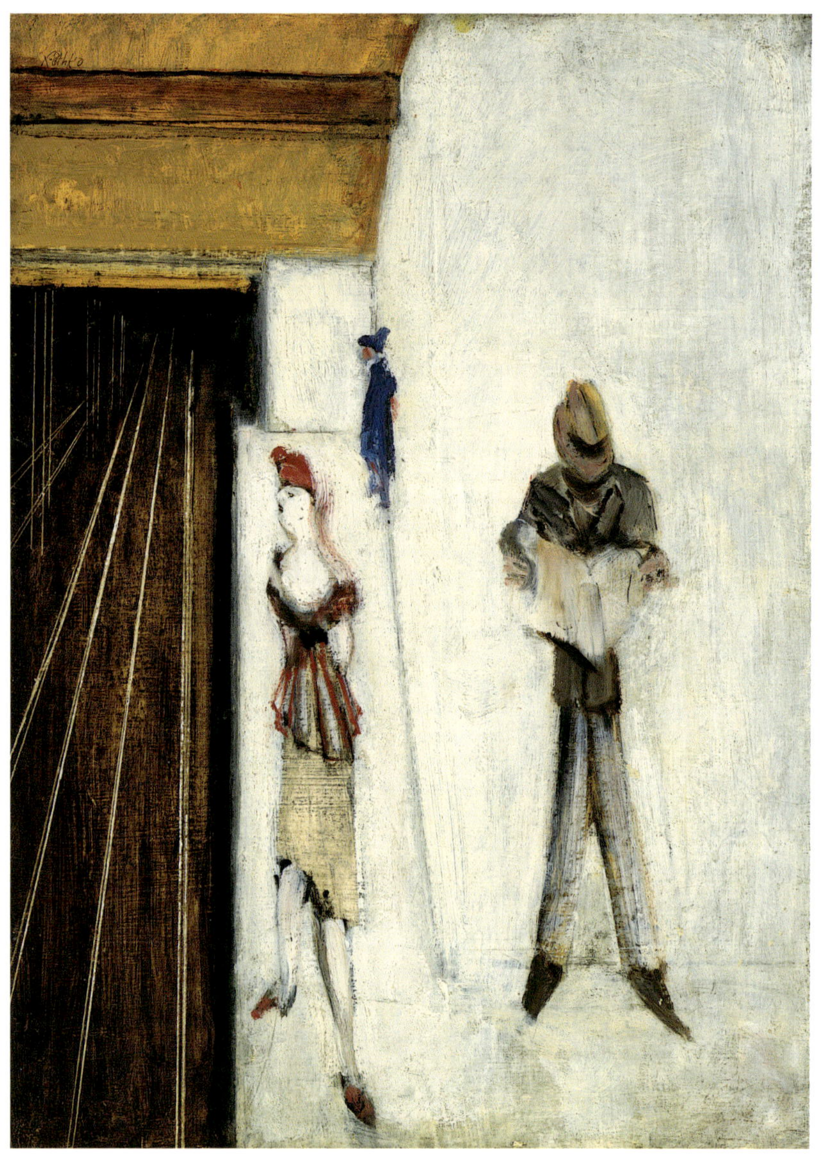

24

15. Untitled (Subway), 1939
oil on gesso board
19 x 14"

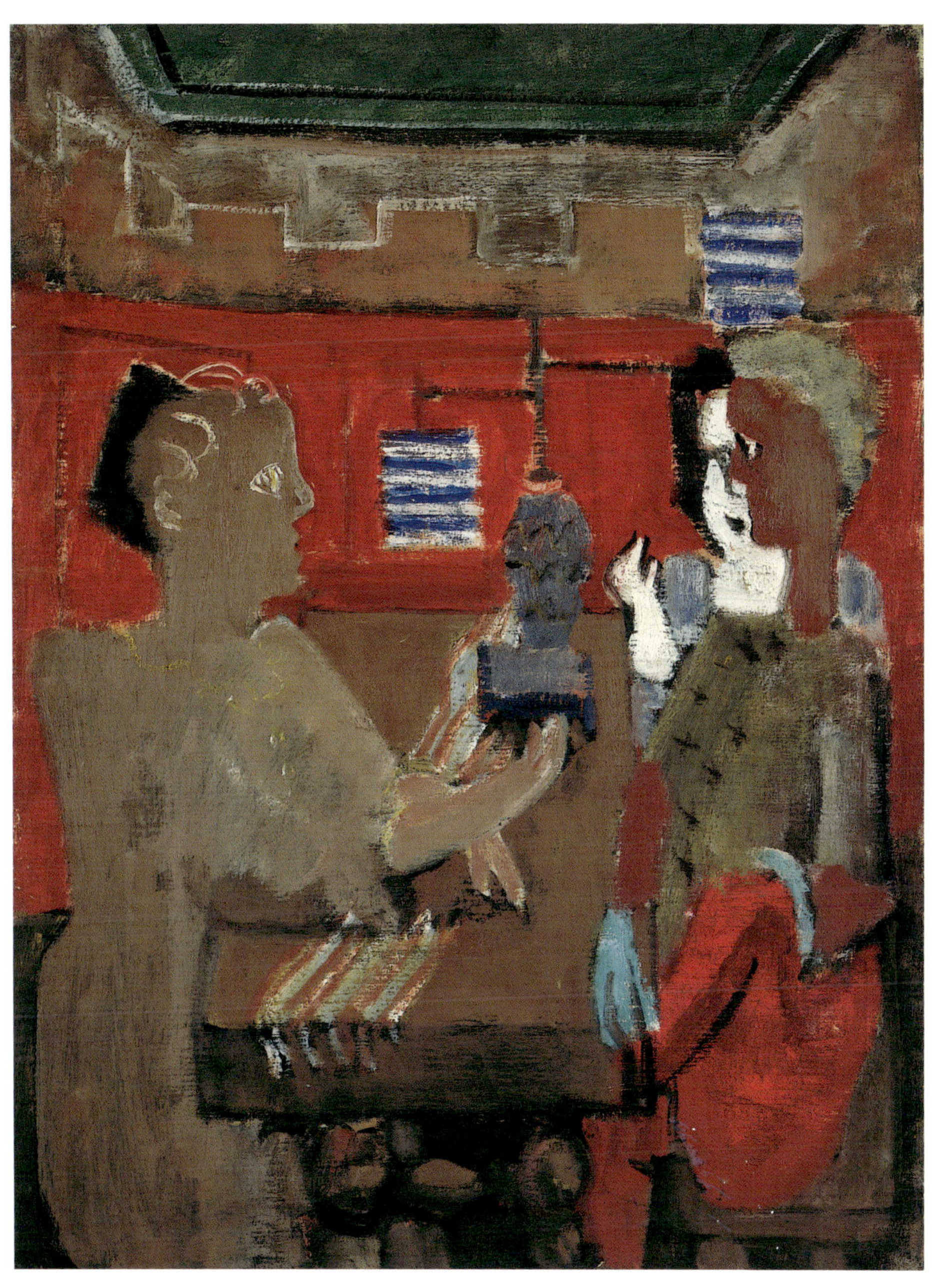

16. Untitled (Three Women Talking), 1938
oil on canvas
32 ⅛ x 24 ¼"

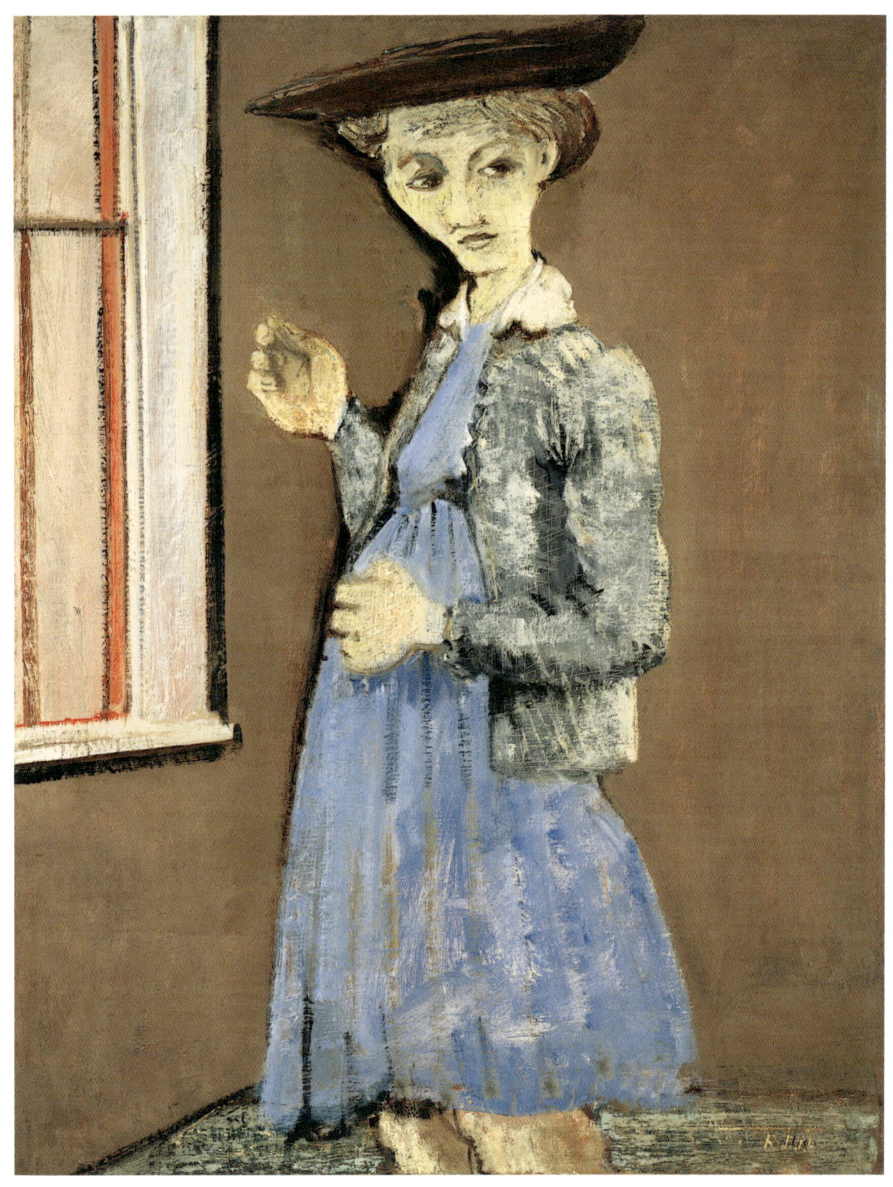

17. Portrait of Mary, 1938-39
oil on canvas
36 x 28 ⅛"

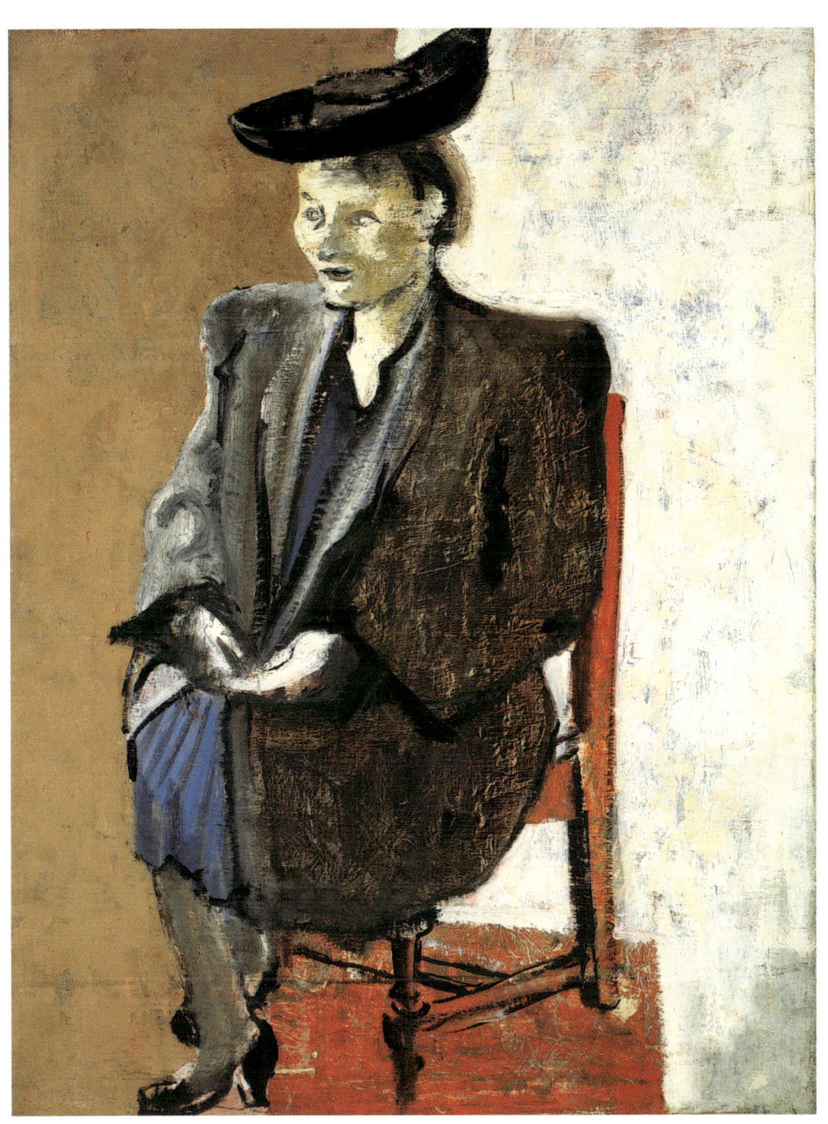

18. Untitled (Seated Woman), 1938
oil on canvas
32 ⅛ x 24 ¼"

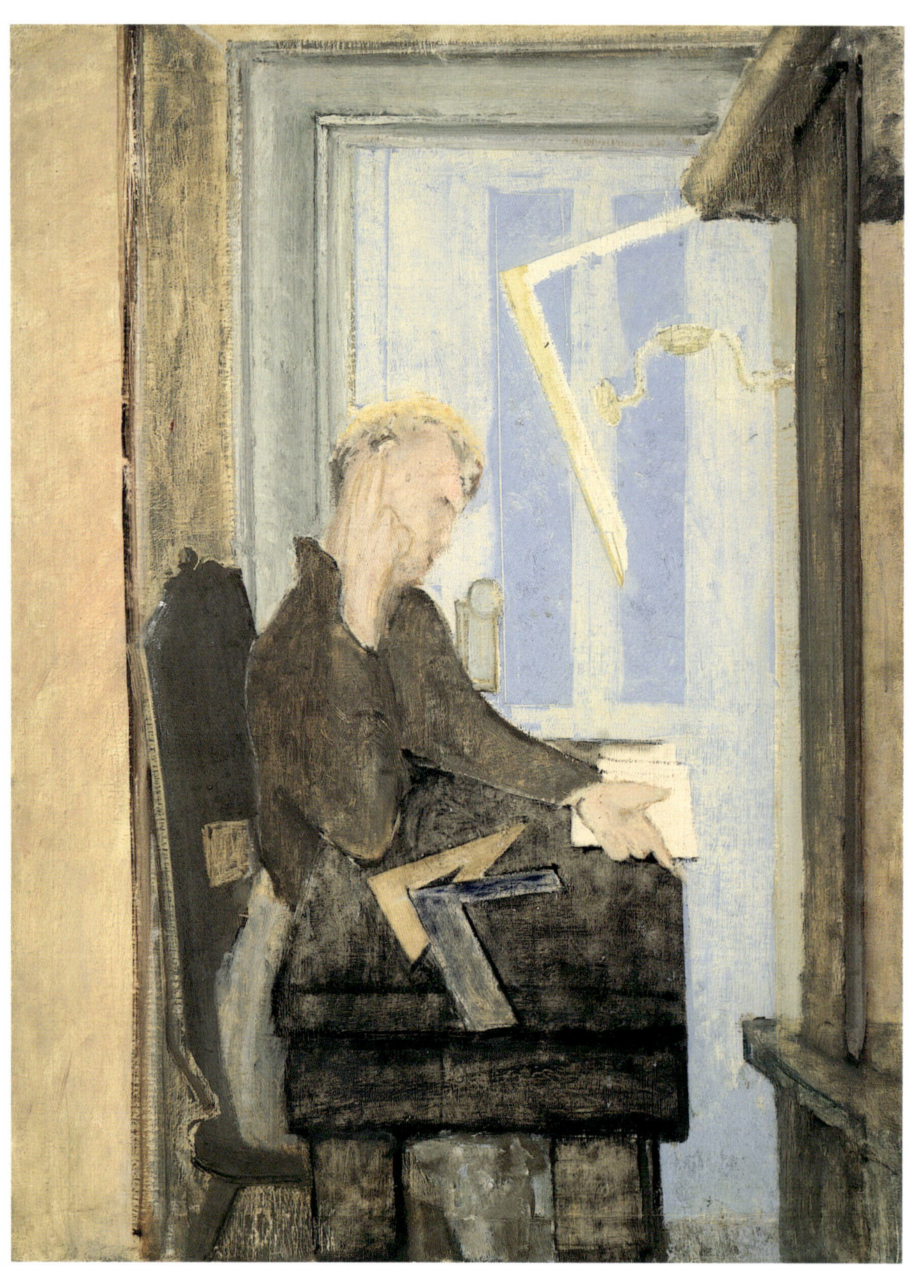

19. Untitled (Seated Man), 1938-39
oil on canvas
40 x 30″

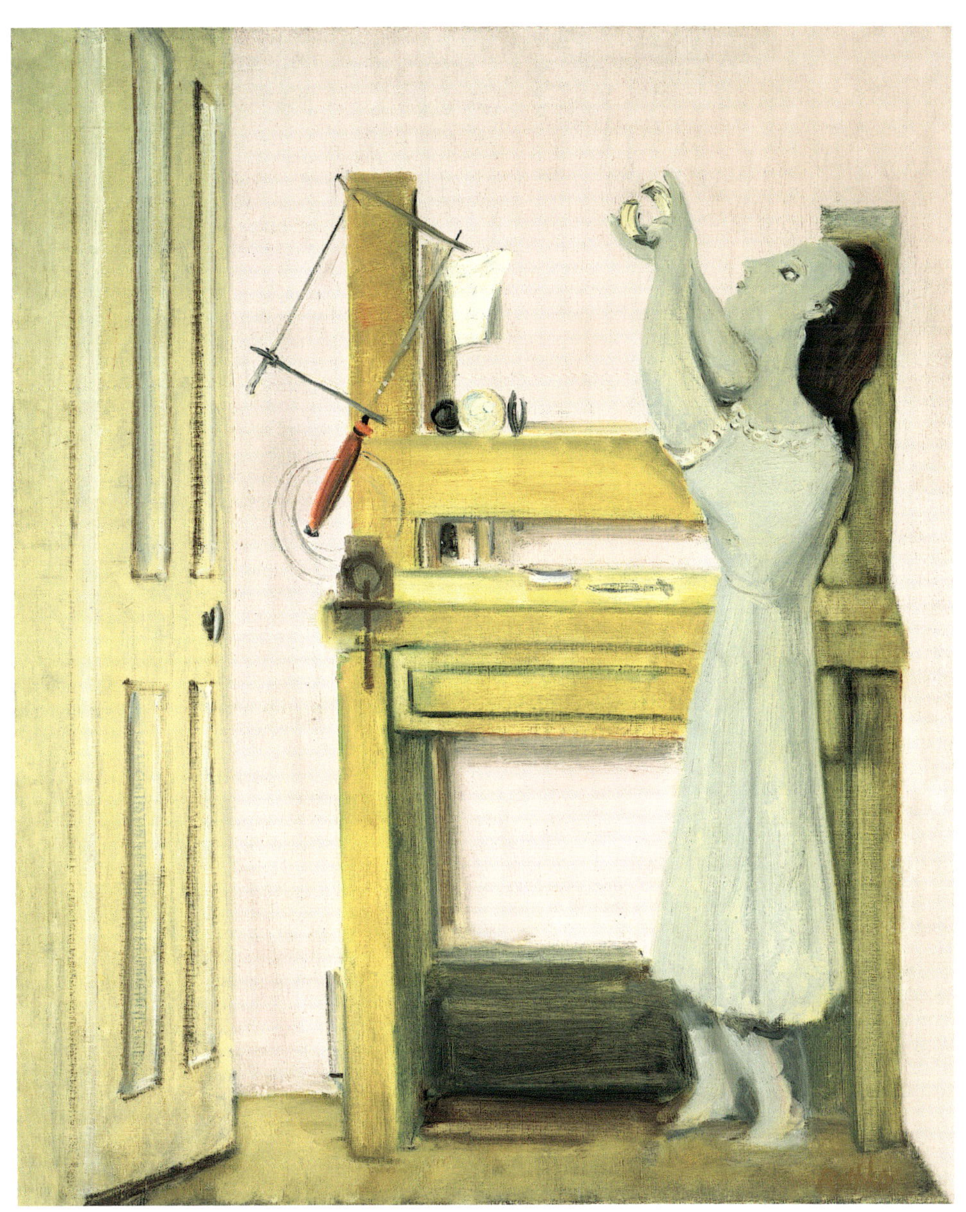

20. Craftsman, 1938-39
oil on linen
36 x 29 $^5/_8$"

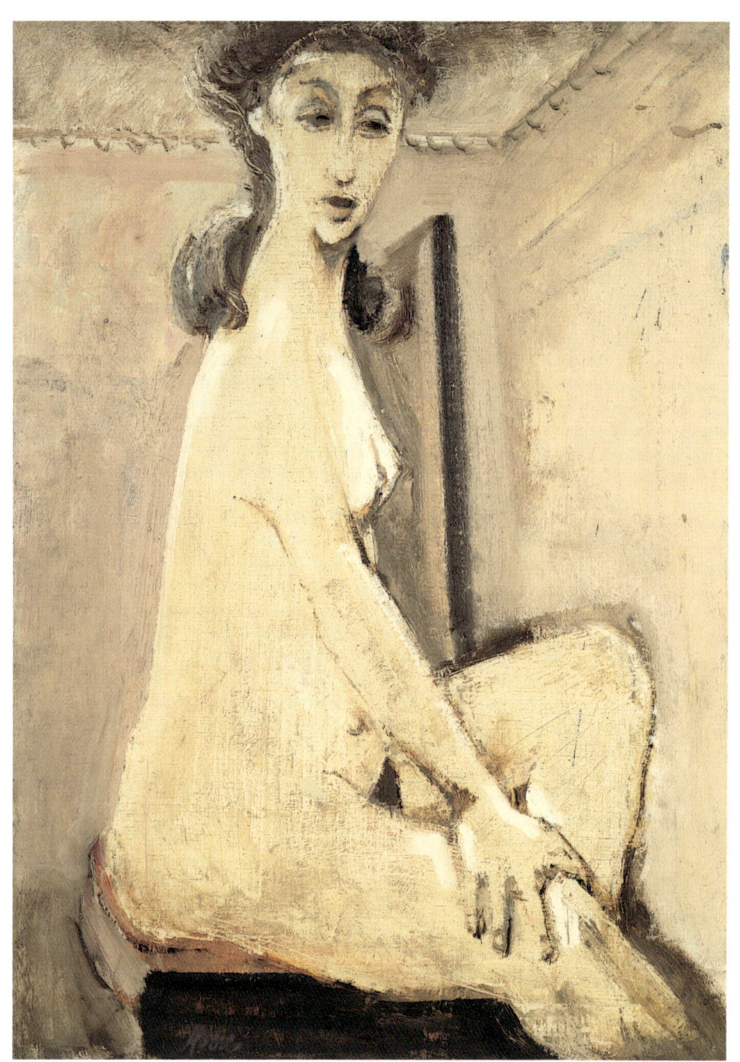

21. Seated Figure, 1939
oil on canvas
28 x 20"

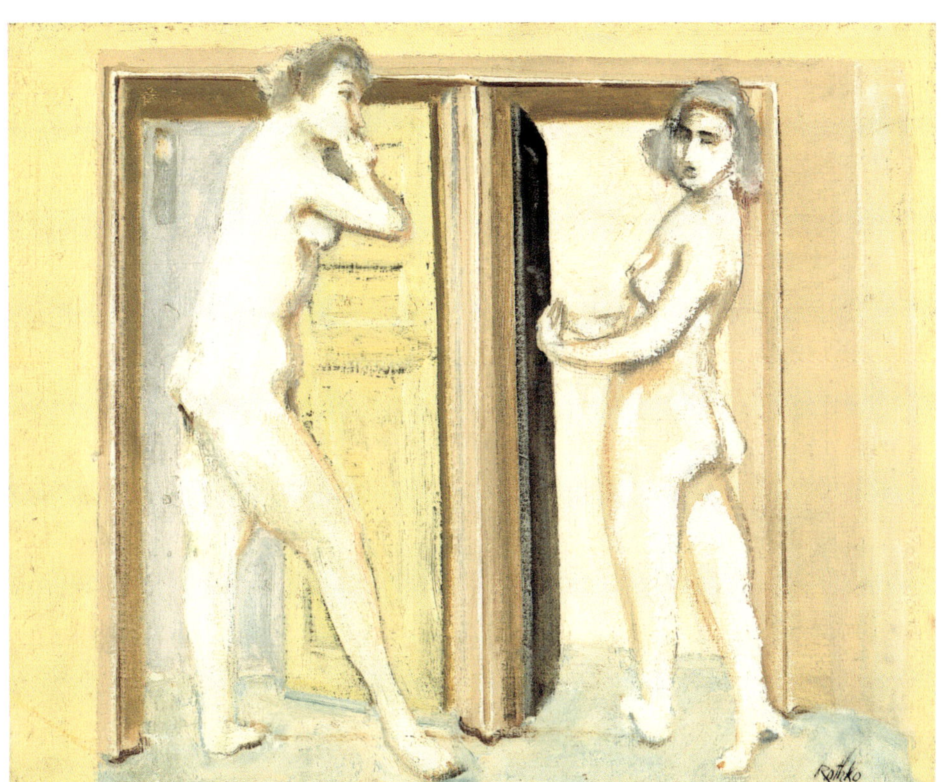

22. Untitled (Two Nudes Standing in Front of a Doorway), 1939
oil on canvas
16 ⅛ x 20″
Collection Neuberger Museum of Art
Purchase College, State University of New York, Gift of The Mark Rothko Foundation, Inc.

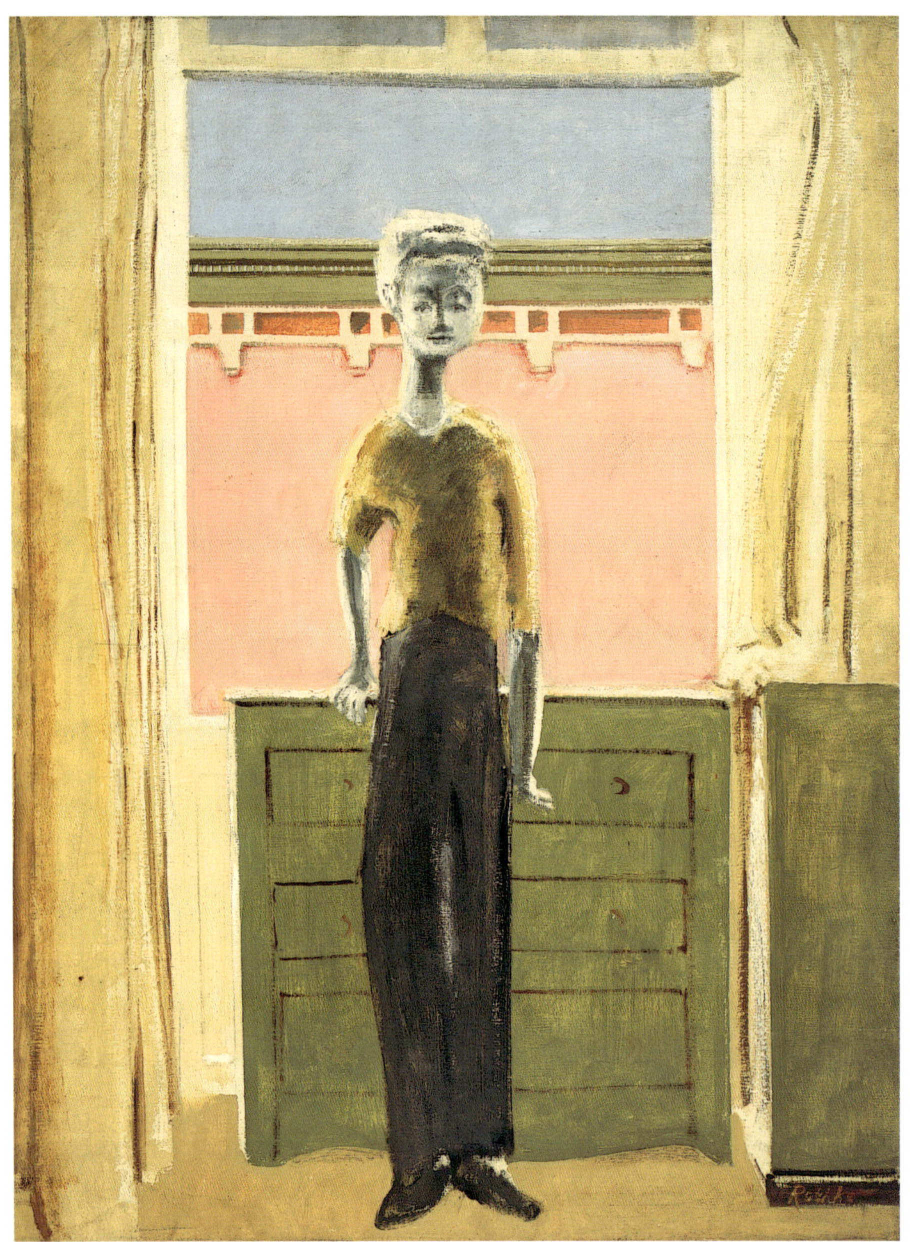

32

23. Untitled (Standing Boy), 1939
oil on canvas
39 ⅞ x 30 ¼"

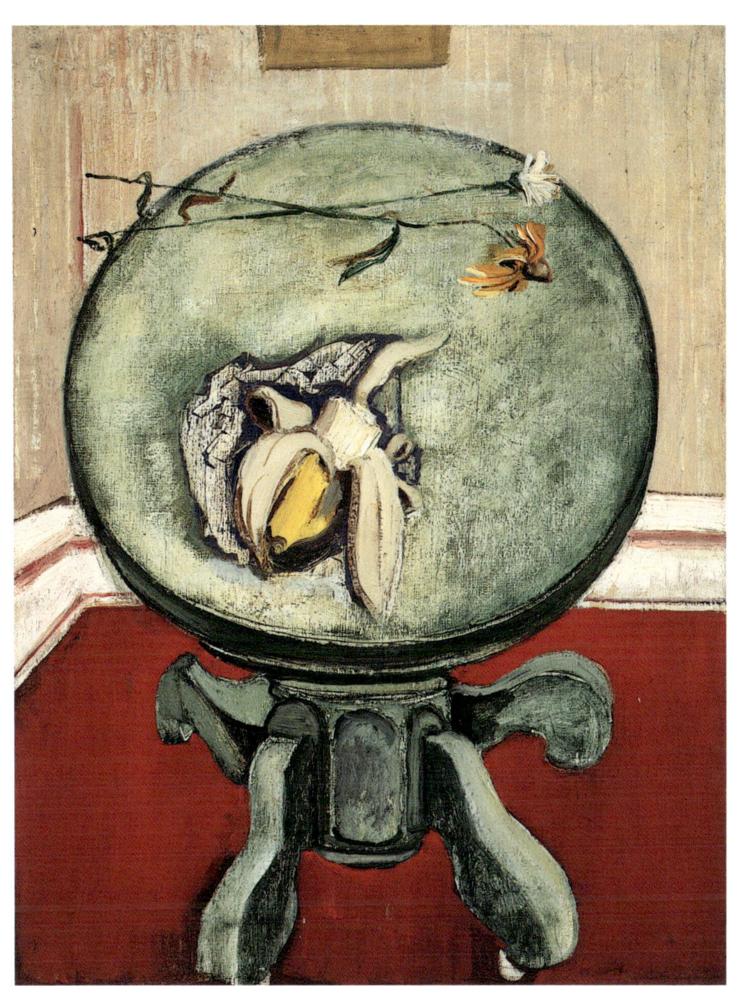

24. Untitled (Still-Life with Two Flowers and Banana), 1939
oil on canvas
24 ⅞ x 19"

1. Untitled (Two Seated Women), 1933-34
oil on black linen
18 ⅝ x 15 ½"
Estate No. 3206.30
Catalog Raisonné No. 51
Lent by the Brooklyn Museum of Art
Gift of The Mark Rothko Foundation, Inc.

2. Bathers, 1933-34 (inscribed on verso "1930-33")
oil on canvas
21 x 27"
Estate No. 3196.30
Catalog Raisonné No. 46

3. The Red Blouse, 1933-34 (inscribed on verso "1930-33")
oil on canvas
31 ½ x 16"
Estate No. 3109.30
Catalog Raisonné No. 43

4. Self-Portrait, 1936
oil on canvas
32 ¼ x 25 ¾"
Estate No. 3266.36
Catalog Raisonné No. 82

5. Untitled (Couple Kissing), 1934-35
oil on canvas
12 ⅛ x 14"
Estate No. 14P
Catalog Raisonné No. 69

6. Untitled (Two Women at a Window), c.1937
oil on canvas
40 x 30"
Collection of Ira Smolin and Linda Washburn
Catalog Raisonné No. 101

7. Interior, 1936
oil on hardboard
23 ⅞ x 18 ¼"
Estate No. 3069.32
Catalog Raisonné No. 79
National Gallery of Art, Washington
Gift of The Mark Rothko Foundation, Inc.

8. Untitled (Lobby/Restaurant), 1936-37
(inscribed on verso "1934-36")
oil on canvas
28 x 36"
Estate No. 3118.34
Catalog Raisonné No. 93

9. Untitled (Waiting Room), 1935
oil on canvas
32 ⅜ x 42"
Estate No. 3018.30
Catalog Raisonné No. 70

10. Subway, c. 1937
oil on canvas
29 ⅞ x 35 ⅞"
Estate No. 3050.38
Catalog Raisonné No. 111

11. Metropolitan Scene, 1934-36
oil on canvas
36 x 22"
Estate No. 3119.34
Catalog Raisonné No. 112

12. Untitled (Subway), 1937
oil on canvas
24 x 36"
Collection of Ira Smolin and Linda Washburn
Catalog Raisonné No. 104

34

13. Subway, 1938-39 (inscribed on verso "1939")
oil on canvas
34 ¼ x 29 ⅞"
Estate No. 3051.39
Catalog Raisonné No. 145

14. Untitled (Woman in Subway), c. 1938
oil on canvas
40 x 30"
Estate No. 3090.36
Catalog Raisonné No. 140

15. Untitled (Subway), 1939
oil on gesso board
19 x 14"
Estate No. 10P
Catalog Raisonné No. 165

16. Untitled (Three Women Talking), 1938
oil on canvas
32 ⅛ x 24 ¼"
Estate No. 3117.34
Catalog Raisonné No. 137

17. Portrait of Mary, 1938-39
oil on canvas
36 x 28 ⅛"
Estate No. 3093.36
Catalog Raisonné No. 157

18. Untitled (Seated Woman), 1938
oil on canvas
32 ⅛ x 24 ¼"
Estate No. 3087.36
Catalog Raisonné No. 136

19. Untitled (Seated Man), 1938-39
oil on canvas
40 x 30"
Estate No. 3091.36
Catalog Raisonné No. 163

20. Craftsman, 1938-39
oil on linen
36 x 29 ⅝"
Estate No. 3094.36
Catalog Raisonné No. 162

21. Seated Figure, 1939 (inscribed on verso "1936-38")
oil on canvas
28 x 20"
Estate No. 3236.36
Catalog Raisonné No. 172

**22. Untitled (Two Nudes Standing in
Front of a Doorway),** 1939
oil on canvas
16 ⅛ x 20"
Collection Neuberger Museum of Art
Purchase College, State University of New York,
Gift of The Mark Rothko Foundation, Inc.
Estate No. 3227.36
Catalog Raisonné No. 173

23. Untitled (Standing Boy), 1939
oil on canvas
39 ⅞ x 30 ¼"
Estate No. 3092.36
Catalog Raisonné No. 164

**24. Untitled (Still-Life with Two
Flowers and Banana),** 1939
(inscribed on verso "1934-36")
oil on canvas
24 ⅞ x 19"
Estate No. 3123.34
Catalog Raisonné No. 169